LAW 4 LAYMAN

Legal Laws in India

Ajit Kumar

Legal Mind

To Contact Ajit Kumar for speaking engagement and coaching, please email:
legalmindajitkumar@gmail.com

SELF-HELP/LEGAL

Published by Legal Mind

ISBN : 978-81-924969-0-0

INTRODUCTION

Laws are intriguing; and conflicting Legal precedence makes it more confusing to be understood by a common man. People want straight answers to the common and not so common legal problems. It is this area, where this book solves the concerns and challenges of a layman. This book is a pocket law for layman.

The book offers clear and concise solution and answers to a variety of legal problems ranging from Family Law to Contract Law and so forth. It also gives latest Supreme Court Judgments on the subject and links to different Legal blogs for further readership. A good Legal Glossary is an added benefit of this book.

I was inspired to write this book, since of late, I have been answering to legal queries through my website, blogs and E-mails, which were raised by people from all walks of life on varying legal aspects. I found that there is a void due to non-availability of a book providing instant answers to some of most common and frequently asked legal questions. What people/readers want is not the complete law but crux of it, clearly elucidating and answering to their legal queries.

Readers will find common legal querries and their answers, Tips, quotes, illustration/examples and latest legal judgments in this book, beside, some of legal formats, Legal Glossary and an Essay on Indian Legal Framework.

This book is a must read for all; be he may a layman, student, researcher, businessman or even a lawyer. I am sure it would be a great learning experience going through this book.

AJIT KUMAR

Author's Note:

The author is a lawyer practicing in India, and also a certified mediator. The author is also serving as a member mediator in court annexed mediation program in Delhi courts. This book is an attempt to explain some of the legal aspects of different laws from the perspective of a layman. The objective of publishing this book is to educate a common man regarding his legal rights, and to enable him to make the best use of legal provisions and legal remedies made available under the law.

The information given in this book is merely for guidance and reference. The author has taken all possible care to bring out the correct position of law in the background of latest apex legal judgments.

CONTENTS

CHAPTER 1

CONSUMER CASES; TORTS (CIVIL WRONGS)

CHAPTER 1

CONSUMER CASES; TORTS (CIVIL WRONGS)

Q1. **If a driver under my employment commits an accident while delivering some important papers to my office. What is my liability in such eventuality as the owner of the car?**

A. Where an employee commits an accident during performance of his duties, the principles of vicarious liability can be invoked. A master is vicariously liable for the acts of his servant done during the course of his employment. The driver of the car delivering some important documents of the master was in fact performing his duties, and thus, renders the master vicariously liable if he commits an accident. However, if the driver commits an accident, and at the time of accident, he is not acting in performance of his duties, but is doing something for himself and without authority of his master, then the master is not liable.

Q2. **A public carrier company has lost goods during transit. The booking receipt says that the company will not be liable for loss of damage. What is the liability of the company and whether a case could be filed for loss of goods?**

A. The liability of a common carrier in India is not only in general for negligence, but they have a special liability as Insurers. A common carrier is not merely a bailee, and his liability against the loss or damage is not confined to Sections 151, 152 and 161 of the **Indian Contract Act, 1872**. He is an insurer of the goods, and in the absence of a special contract with the owner of goods; his liability is absolute. The note on the booking receipt does not absolve the carrier company from its liability to the owner of the goods for the loss occasioned during transit.

Q3. What is medical negligence? What is the standard of care expected of a doctor in India?

A. It is a result of breach of duty owed by the doctor towards his patient to exercise reasonable care and skill, which may lead to some physical, mental or financial disability. The duties which a doctor owes to his patients have been enumerated by Honourable Supreme court **(Case: L.B. Joshi vs. T.B. Godbole, AIR 1969 SC 131**).

"…. a person, who holds himself out to give medical advice and treatment, implicitly undertakes that he is possessed of the skill and knowledge for the purpose. Such a person, when consulted by a patient, owes him certain duties, viz-a-viz a duty of care in deciding whether to undertake the case; a duty to care in deciding what treatment to given or a duty of care in the administration of that treatment. A breach of any of those duties gives a right of action for negligence to the patient. The practitioner must bring to his task a reasonable degree of skill and knowledge, and must exercise a reasonable degree of care. Neither, the highest degree of care is required, nor is the lowest degree of care enough. What is required is a reasonable degree of care and competence, judged in the light of the circumstances of the case."

Q4. **"A" had purchased a truck and the same was to be used for self employment and for his livelihood. There was an inherent manufacturing defect, which was not rectified by the company. Can a consumer complaint be filed before consumer forum?**

A. The act is not applicable for commercial transactions. Therefore, complainant who obtains goods for commercial purpose is not a "consumer" within the definition under Consumer Protection Act and is not entitled to maintain a consumer complaint. **(1991 CPC 155 Del.)**. However, the truck purchased by complainant for self employment can't be termed as a commercial transaction, and a consumer complaint is maintainable. **(1995 (2) CPC 2 SC)**

CHAPTER 2

COMMERCIAL CONTRACT

CHAPTER 2

COMMERCIAL CONTRACT

Q1. **A contract was signed at Mumbai; however, the said contract was to be performed at Patna. The offer for the contract was made at Delhi. Can I file a suit for breach of terms of the contract at Delhi?**

A. A contract is concluded when the offer is accepted and/or contract is signed. Therefore, a suit for breach of contract can be filed either at the place where it is signed, and executed or at the place where it has to be performed and the breach occurred. The cause of action/ place of suing can't be based merely on the place of offer; however, suit can be filed at a place where such offer has been accepted.

Q2. **An oral agreement to sell was entered into between the parties for sale and purchase of a house, and in furtherance of which earnest money was paid. Whether such an oral agreement can be specifically enforced in court by filing a suit for specific performance?**

A. Yes, oral agreement is recognized by law, and is equally enforceable as a written agreement is. The important ingredient for a concluding contract is that parties must be ad-idem, and there should be meeting of minds. Although, in enforcement of an oral agreement it is always difficult to prove creation of such an agreement, but a suit based on oral agreement to sell is equally maintainable in law.

Q3. **I entered into a registered agreement to purchase a house and the seller was under contractual obligation to surrender possession of the house on the execution of agreement to purchase and receipt of the earnest money. The seller did not give the possession of the house after the contract was concluded and earnest money paid. What legal action can I take?**

A. In view of the written registered agreement, the other party is obliged to perform his part of contract and failure of the same, entitles you to seek for specific performance of the agreement, and in alternative for refund of money paid by you to the seller. In case, you are not interested in buying the house after the breach of contract by the seller, you have the option open to file a suit for refund of earnest money and damages.

Q4. **Whether or not, a promise to marry someone can be enforced by one against the other party from the court of law? My boy friend promised to marry me, but has changed his mind. Is it a breach of contract?**

A. In India, the law relating to promise to marry is not express in our statue. However, as far as common Law is concerned, promise to marry can be enforced, breach of which calls for specific performance and claim for damages. Offer and acceptance are the two fundamental elements of the promise to marry agreement.

A promise to marry, if accepted, becomes a contract, which may have a lawful consideration with lawful object. In the claim for specific performance, the court may say that the promisor and promisee should get married. However, such relief is complex as the enforcement of it is troublesome. Therefore, the practice has shown that courts are often than not reluctant in granting such a relief. Court can also grant damages to the successful party for the breach of promise to marry as long as the promise does not infringe on public policy or morals. The grant of damages could be general or special; however, courts are reluctant in granting punitive damages, since the idea is to compensate, and not to levy penalty.

Q5. **The banks recovery agent has towed away a vehicle on account of default of a couple of EMI's. The concerned party has offered to pay the defaulted installments, but the bankers have refused to return the vehicle. They have informed in writing that the vehicle has been auctioned, and are demanding payment of the remaining loan amount. Kindly, advice the legal options available to the owner of the vehicle?**

A. The owner can file a suit for recovery of car, or in the alternative for damages suffered due to sale of the vehicle without prior knowledge of the owner. The owner can also approach banking ombudsman, in case the vehicle is registered in individual name by filing a complaint against the bank. The bank has no right to sell the car without giving a notice to the owner, and also an opportunity to pay the defaulted EMI's.

CHAPTER 3

NEGOTIABLE INSTRUMENT (CHEQUE BOUNCING)

CHAPTER 3

NEGOTIABLE INSTRUMENT (CHEQUE BOUNCING)

Q1. A cheque issued by an individual person (drawer) has been dishonoured for "Insufficient Funds" or alike reasons. What legal action I can take against the drawer of the cheque?

A. The dishonourment of a cheque gives the drawee or the holder in due course a right to recover the amount by filing a suit for recovery of the cheque amount along with costs & interest under Order 37 CPC (under summary provision). In addition to which, after issuance of a written statutory notice to the drawer of the cheque, he can also file a criminal complaint u/s 138 of Negotiable Instrument Act for punishment to the signatory of the cheque for the offence. The statutory notice must be issued within 30 days from date of knowledge of dishonourment of the cheque. The accrual of cause of action for filing the criminal complaint starts on the expiry of the 15th day, upon failure of the drawer to pay the cheque amount (after the due service of the statutory notice). The said complaint should be filed within one month on the accrual of cause of action.

Q2. A notice was served to the drawer upon dishonour of a cheque; however, no complaint under Sec. 138 of Negotiable Instrument Act, 1881 was filed within stipulated period. Is a complaint based on second notice maintainable?

A. A complaint based upon a second notice is not maintainable in the ordinary course; however, if the first notice was not served upon the drawer, the complaint on the basis of the second notice would be maintainable under the Negotiable Instrument Act. I would like to further elaborate that the cause of action for filing a complaint accrues only once, and that is on the failure of the drawer to pay the cheque amount within 15 days of the receipt of the notice. Therefore, if the party has failed to take action by filing complaint with in stipulated period after the cause of action arose based on first notice, a second notice would not give a fresh cause of action and subsequent complaint would not be maintainable.

The combined reading of sub-section 2 of the proviso to Sec.138 and Sec. 142 of the Act leaves no room for doubt that cause of action within the meaning of S.142 accrues and accrues only once. Therefore, a complaint under Sec. 138 r/w 142 of Negotiable Instrument Act, based on second notice is not valid. **(YOGINDER KR.SHARMA VS. ASHOK KUMAR SHARMA; 1999 IV AD (DELHI) 357)**

Q3. Can a notice be given under Negotiable

Instrument Act demanding more than dishonoured cheque amount, which may include interest, costs etc. Whether such a notice is valid and legal?

A. Sections 138, 139 of Negotiable Instrument Act, 1881 require notice of demand to be issued to the drawer of the cheque. However, the words "said amount of money" in clause (b) and (c) to proviso to Sec.138 refers to amount of money under the cheque. Therefore, in notice, under clause (b) to the proviso, demand has to be made for the cheque amount

However, where in addition to cheque amount, there is also a claim by way of interest; costs etc., validity of the notice would depend on its language. If in a notice, while giving break up of claim the cheque amount, interest, damages etc. are separately specified, then these additional claims for interest, costs etc. being superfluous and severable, will not invalidate the notice. If, however, in the notice an omnibus demand is made without specifying what was due under the dishonored cheque, notice may be regarded as bad. The Object of notice is to give a chance to drawer to rectify his omission and not to penalize. If cheque amount is paid within the period of 15 days or before complaint is filed, legal liability u/s. 138 will cease. **(SUMAN SETHI VS. AJAY K. CHURIWAL ; 2000 (1) SCALE 385)**

CHAPTER 4

ESTATE MANAGEMENT (WILL, PROBATE & SUCCESSION CERTIFICATE; RIGHT OF INHERITANCE)

CHAPTER 4

ESTATE MANAGEMENT (WILL, PROBATE & SUCCESSION CERTIFICATE; RIGHT OF INHERITANCE)

Q1. **What is the meaning of nominee? Does nominee have any preferential rights over the legal heirs of deceased for a LIC policy?**

A. Nominee is a person who can give a valid discharge for receiving the benefits under nomination and acts as a trustee to the legal heirs/beneficiaries entitled to receive the same under Law. Thus, legal heirs still hold charge over the benefits and are entitled to claim back the benefits from the nominee, subject to his/her own Share, in case the nominee is also a legal heir. A mere nomination made under Sec. 39 Insurance Act does not have the effect of conferring on the nominee any preferential interest in the amount payable under the Life Insurance Policy. **(AIR 1991 SC 392; LIC Vs. G.M. Channabasemma)**

Q2. **What is Hindu undivided family Property? Whether a grandson has an independent right to the self acquired property of the grandfather, even if he has executed a will in favour of his sons? What would be the position in case grandfather having ancestral property viz.-a-viz., the rights of the grandson in the**

said property?

A. A Hindu undivided Family property is a property jointly owned and possessed by a joint Hindu family with male lineal decedents having coparcenary rights in the joint property. Grand Son has no right by his birth in the self acquired property of his grand-father unless one of the conditions are fulfilled, which are:-

a) If the self acquired property of the grand father is got converted into joint family property of the Hindu undivided Family by putting the self acquired property into hotch-potch with the intention to divest his right in the said property, which is called "doctrine of Blending"; or

b) If the grand father has declared in the will the beneficiary (father) shall be receiving the property as an ancestral property.

Grandfather is competent to give his self acquired property to his son by bequeathing the same by a will. However, in what manner it is coming in the hands of the father (as ancestral or separate/ individual) would be governed by the language and the intention of the executor of the will i.e., Grand father.

On the other hand, in case of ancestral property, the grandson acquires a right in the property of his grandfather at his birth and has a right of inheritance jointly with his father at the time of succession. If the property is an ancestral then no will can be made limiting or extinguishing the right of the grandson, who has a right to claim his share in the ancestral property.

Q3. What is a will? How to make a will and register it?

A. Will is a testamentary document making a self declaration of the intention of a person with respect to his property or an estate, which he desires to be carried out after his death. Such legal declaration comes into force after the death of a person making the deposition and therefore, it is a document which can be revoked, modify or substituted by the person executing the will at any point of his time during his life time.

The principal requirements for executing a will are:

a). It should be in writing (the will of a Muslim can be oral);

b). It must bear the signature of the testator; and

c). It must be attested by at least two witnesses.

Beside, for executing the will the person must be fully competent i.e., he should not be a minor and should not be person of unsound mind. The will under law is not required to be compulsory registered. It can be executed even on a plain paper; however, it is always advisable to register it with Sub-registrar. The Sub-registrar would be as per the place of the residence of the person executing the will.

Q4. What is the purpose of making a will and what would be the right time to make a will?

A. The purpose of making a will is to be in control of your assets and to bequeath it as per your desire. One can be in control of his assets by executing a will in his lifetime. It is said that prevention is better than cure and therefore, to avoid litigation for inheritance of your property amongst surviving legal heirs, one must make a will in his/her life time.

Example:

I had this case, which was handled in Delhi High Court of a senior citizen relating to a south Delhi prime property, where the father died intestate (without a will) and all three brothers had came up with their own version of will allegedly executed by father, when father had executed none.

Q5. Can I make my will only in the name of my son to the exclusion of my daughters? Also if a person dies without making a will then are daughters entitled to have right in the property?

A Yes, you can make will exclusively in favour of your son by excluding the daughters. If no will is made, your property shall be inherited in equal share by all the legal heirs, which include daughters also.

CHAPTER 5 RENT MATTERS

CHAPTER 5

RENT MATTERS (LANDLORD AND TENANT DISPUTES)

Q1. **Can an eviction petition on the ground of bonafide necessity be filed for commercial tenancy also? I had filed an eviction petition on the ground of bonafide necessity of my dependent son, who needs the shop for establishing his business. Whether, such a bonafide necessity for a dependent son is justified?**

A. Yes, recently in **Satyawati Sharma Vs. Union of India; 148 (2008) DLT 705 (SC)**, (see article at *http://advocateajitkumar.blogspot.com*) the Hon'ble Supreme Court has held that even commercial tenancy comes within the purview of the section 14 (1) (e) of Delhi Rent Act, 1958. The son being dependent upon father/landlord, such a demand is justified. This ground of eviction is governed by the summary procedure provided under Sec.25-B of the Delhi Rent Act, 1958. The ground is justified and eviction can be sought by proving the ground of bone fide requirement.

Q2. **Can a civil suit for eviction be filed against the tenant by the landlord, if the monthly rent**

is Rs. 3,000/- ?

A. No, Sec. 50 of Delhi Rent Control Act, 1958 clearly bars a suit for eviction of a tenant or any thing ancillary to the said tenancy and thus, the civil court has no jurisdiction to try and adjudicate such a suit for eviction of a tenant. The Non-obstante clause of Sec.3 (c) of the Act says that no provision of the Rent Act shall apply to premises who's rent exceed Rs.3500/-. The cumulative effect of Sec.50 and Sec.3 (c) clearly bars the jurisdiction of a civil court. The landlord must plead and prove one of the grounds mentioned under Sec.14(1) of the Delhi Rent Control Act, before a rent controller. A petition for eviction under Delhi Rent Act, 1958 alone is maintainable before a rent controller of the concerned district, where the tenanted premises is situated.

Q3. **I am one of the co-owner of a property, which was let out by me. The tenant has stopped paying the rent, but the other co-owners of the property are not interested in filing any case for the recovery of the arrears. Can I file a case for recovery of my share of the arrears of rent and/or for his eviction?**

A. A Co-owner has joint ness in ownership and possession and therefore, he is owner of each and every inch of the property. Thus, he is also entitled to terminate lease and to file suit for possession solely, however, he may include the other Co-owners, as defendants along with the tenant. The option is available to a co-owner to pray for a decree for his share of arrears of rent by filing a suit on the basis of unity of interest in the tenancy/ tenanted premises and without splitting the same. However, it is not necessary for a co-owner to sue for the entire arrears of rent to maintain a case for recovery of rent and he can claim his share of rent from the tenant.

Q4. A portion of my house was let out by me to a tenant for one year but the written lease was unregistered and I have been accepting rent from him. The lease period has expired, as mentioned in the lease deed. Is a notice necessary for evicting my tenant?

A. A tenant continuing to occupy the tenanted premises after expiry of lease by efflux of time and paying rent to the landlord became a `tenant holding over'. Such a tenancy becomes a month to month tenancy, which can be terminated (in case of lease other than for Industrial/factory purpose) by giving a clear 15 days notice under Sec.106 of Transfer of Property Act. Since, in the present case the written lease was unregistered and therefore, the terms of lease are inadmissible in evidence. Therefore, a notice under Section 106 of the Transfer of Property Act is mandatory for initiating eviction proceeding against the tenant.

Q5. An Individual tenancy was created in favour of "A" and rent was being paid by him, however, later "A" was joined by other persons and a Partnership Firm came into existence with "A", as one of the partner. The rent was

tendered by the Partnership Firm and was accepted by the Landlord. Whether a tenancy has been created in favour of Partnership Firm?

A. Mere payment and acceptance of rent does create tenancy. Tenancy is created by a contract either written or oral. (SHYAM KISHORE V/S. UNION OF INDIA; 59 (1995) DLT 416(DB) = 1995 (25) RLR 480). Merely because a Partnership firm consisting of the individual "A" has been created with some other partners and rent has been paid by the said firm, tenancy is not transferred or created in the name of partnership firm. The partnership firm can not be held as a tenant.

Q6. **I am tenant in a property with the new owner having a disputed title. However, even after it came to my knowledge about his disputed ownership; I continued to pay monthly rent to him. Is mere acceptance of rent sufficient to make a person landlord?**

A. In view of definition clause under Sec.2 (e) of Delhi Rent Act, a Landlord is the person who is entitled and has the right to receive rent. Mere acceptance of rent does not make a person landlord unless he has the legal right to receive the rent. Although, a tenant is estopped under Sec.116 of Indian Evidence Act, to challenge the title, how so ever, defective it may be of the landlord who has inducted him as a tenant. However, in the present case, title can be challenged by the tenant of a subsequent purchaser of the property, who has a defective/ disputed title.

Q7. During pendency of an eviction proceeding under Rent Control Act, if there are arrears of rent should the controller direct the tenant to pay such arrears prior to allowing the tenant to contest the case further?

A. If the eviction petition is on the ground of non payment of rent then the rent controller is under duty to pass an order for deposit of rent u/s 15 (1) of Delhi Rent Control Act. It has been held, that the passing of interim order under Sec. 15(1) of the DRC Act, is not only for the benefit of the landlord but also for the tenant. If the eviction petition is based on any other ground then you have to make an application under Section 15 (2) of Delhi Rent Control Act for direction to the tenant to deposit the rent. If no rent is deposited as per order of the court, the court has the right to strike off the defense of the tenant.

Q8. What should I do to ensure a safe recovery of my property, if I let it out to a tenant? The rent would be around Rs.10,000/- per month.

A. The object of the most of the provisions of Delhi Rent Control Act, 1958 was to give a protective umbrella against arbitrary actions of the landlord for eviction of tenants. However, Sec. 3 (c) was incorporated after the amendment made in the Delhi Rent Control Act by a repealing act in the year 1988. The provision was made that in case the rent of the premises is in excess Rs. 3,500/-, the protection against eviction available under the provisions of the Delhi Rent Control Act, 1958 would not to be available to the tenant. The landlord can recover the premises under common law i.e., Transfer of Property Act by filing a civil suit for recovery of possession.

Nothing gives 100% surety or safety, however, such terms in the lease, like keeping adequate amount of security money (interest free) and hefty compensation amount for overstay after expiry of lease would give you adequate leverage to negotiate with the tenant for getting it vacated. However, in case the tenant refuses to vacate, you have no option but to approach the court for recovery of possession and damages from the tenant. Since, the rent is above Rs.3500/-, the tenant is not entitled to the protection under Delhi Rent Control Act.

Further, if the lease is to be executed for a period of one year or more, the same is also compulsorily registrable under Sec.17 of Indian Registration Act, otherwise, the terms of the lease cannot be read in evidence in the court, except for collateral purpose. The precaution, which can be taken by getting a legally drafted lease and its registration, shall help you in recovering the property from the court of law with appropriate damages.

Q.9. **The Landlord is not accepting rent tendered to him personally with the intention to create a ground for eviction on default in payment of rent. What should I do?**

A. As per Sec.26(1) of Delhi Rent Act, the tenant is obliged to pay monthly rent in terms of the written lease and in the absence of that he must pay monthly rent due by the 15th day of next calendar month for which rent is due and payable. Failure of which, he shall liable to pay

15% interest and may suffer eviction for default of payment of rent.

It has been held in recent High Court judgment that the interest accrued under Sec. 26(1) of the Delhi Rent Act, 1958 becomes part of rent and default of it would entail eviction of the tenant. (**Ramprakash vs. D.N. Srivastava; 2006 II AD (DEL) 182=126 (2006) DLT 6)**. Therefore, you must tender rent including arrears with interest by sending a money order to the landlord and on its refusal deposit the same with the rent controller under Sec.27 of the Act by filing a petition for deposit of rent.

CHAPTER 6

MARRIAGE AND DIVORCE, MAINTENANCE OF WIFE AND CHILDREN, MAINTENANCE OF PARENTS AND CUSTODY OF CHILDREN.

CHAPTER 6

MARRIAGE AND DIVORCE; MAINTENANCE OF WIFE AND CHILDREN, MAINTENANCE OF PARENTS, CUSTODY OF CHILDREN

Q1. What does cruelty to married women means and which section is applicable?

A. When a women is subjected to cruelty by her husband or by any relative of the husband, Sec. 498A of code of criminal procedure comes into play. This sec. 498-A of Criminal Procedure Code was inserted by IInd amendment Act, 1983. In such case, one can approach D.C.P (Women Cell) and complain against cruelty for dowry demand under sec. 498-A Cr.P.C. A separate divorce petition could also be filed in the matrimonial court.

Q2. Whether an unmarried financially independent daughter is under legal obligation to maintain her parents? What are the relevant provisions of law applicable?

A. There can be no doubt that it is the moral obligation of a son or a daughter to maintain his or her parents. The statutory provision providing maintenance is Sec.125 (1) (d) of Cr.P.C. In the said provision, the expression used is 'his father or mother' but, the use of the word 'his' does not exclude the parents claiming maintenance from their daughter. (**Bhagwan Dutt Vs. Kamla Devi; 1975 (2) SCC 386**).

Similarly, there are other provisions like section 20 of the Hindu Adoption & Maintenance Act, 1956, which provides for maintenance of the children and aged parents. Under the provisions of the said section, a Hindu is bound, during his or her life time, to maintain his or her legitimate or illegitimate children and his or her aged or infirm parents. A daughter after her marriage does not cease to be a daughter of the father or mother. The Hon'ble Supreme Court therefore has held in **Dr. (Mrs.) Vijaya Manohar Arbat Vs. Kashi Rao Rajaram Sawai & Ors.; 1987 SCR (2) 331** that a daughter, whether married or not, is under an obligation to maintain her parents (i.e. provide for them) as per the provisions of section 125 of Code of Criminal Procedure, who are unable to maintain themselves because of their age or financial incapacity.

Q3. **I am a 35 year old married woman. For two years I am living separately from my husband. My husband has forcibly taken over four year old son with him. The husband is a drunkard and cannot take care of our son. What should I do?**

A. When Child of the family are taken out of home, it becomes an act of inter-parental kidnapping. You can file an application in the court for custody of your son on the plea that it would not be in the welfare of the child, as your husband is a drunkard. In view of the fact that the paramount consideration is the welfare of the child and as, you have not been claiming maintenance of the child, the said fact would show that you can maintain the child of your own and is thus, rightful person to be given custody of the child. The court will take into account to which parent the child is deeply attached, which parent is in a better position to bring up the child properly, what are the facilities available for looking after the child, and so on. If the child is old enough to express its preference, the court will also take into account that preference, though the court is not bound to allow the petition on that basis itself.

Q4. **I am a Hindu Boy and want to marry a Christian girl. How is it possible?**

A. A marriage between couples professing different religion could be registered under ***Special Marriage Act***, and that does not require you to change your religion. However, in case either of you want to change and adopt the religion of the other party, your marriage can be registered under your respective Marriage Act. (Visit at: ***http://lawyerajit.blogspot.com***)

Q5. **My friend got married 6 months back, however, due to differences both of them wants to go for mutual divorce? Is it possible to apply for divorce right now?**

A. Under Section 14 of the Hindu Marriage Act, 1955, no petition for dissolution of marriage by divorce can be filed before the expiry of statutory period of one year of its solemnization. But in case, where the petitioner shall suffer exceptional hardship or of exceptional depravity on the part of the respondent, the court can, in accordance with High Court Rules, grant leave to file the case before the expiry of one year.

Q6. **In a Hindu marriage, the wife started living separately with separate kitchen in the same house for more than one year due to temperamental differences. Whether a joint petition for divorce by mutual consent can be filed? How to proceed with it? When can a person marry again after obtaining a decree of divorce?**

A. A Divorce by mutual consent can be obtained by Husband and Wife in terms of Section 13 B of the Hindu Marriage Act, 1955. The prerequisite for a mutual consent divorce petition under the provisions of the said Section is that the couple must be living separately for a period of more than 1 year and they are not able to live together any further. "Living Separately" has been now defined by the Hon'ble Supreme Court in **(Smt. Sureshta Devi Vs. Om Prakash; 1991 SCC (2) 25 =JT 1991 (1) 321=1991 SCALE (1)156)** as "not living as husband and wife and not performing marital obligations", even if the husband and wife are living under the same roof.

Therefore, as aforesaid, a joint petition (First Motion) can be filed and upon giving consent statement in the first motion the Court grants a minimum period of six months (and maximum 18 months) for filing second motion petition, thereby confirming the said consent. It is only after the consent given by both the parties in second motion petition after six months of the filing of the first motion petition for mutual divorce, that a decree for divorce is passed by the Court. The mutual consent for divorce must continue and extend during the entire period of six months between First Motion and Second Motion Petition till divorce decree is passed. The withdrawal of consent by either party after the filing of the first motion petition and before consent given in second Motion petition would result in denial of granting a divorce decree. Further, apart from the aforesaid, the court shall also satisfy that the consent has not been obtained by force, fraud or undue influence before passing of Divorce Decree. As far as re-marriage after divorce is concerned, Section 15 of the Hindu Marriage Act, 1955, provides that after a decree of divorce has been granted, in case there is no right of appeal against the decree or if there is a right; and the time has expired without an appeal having been presented or if the appeal filed has been dismissed, it shall be lawful for either party to marry again. The period of appeal is 30 days from the date of decree or order in terms of Sec.28 of the Hindu Marriage Act, 1955.

Q7. If the wife has left the house of her husband and was living away from him without any reasonable cause, can the husband be entitled to judicial separation or divorce? Is there any time limit for filing of divorce petition on the ground of desertion?

A. Where the wife has left the house of the husband of her own and is living away from him without any plausible reason for a continuous period of two years, the husband is entitled to judicial separation or divorce on the ground of desertion. The wife must be `living seperately' for a continuous period, which is not less than 2 years, expiring at the time of filing petition for grant of divorce or judicial separation. Thus, the desertion must be continuous and the period of desertion required for filing a divorce petition is at least two years.

Q8. How is "judicial separation" different from "divorce"?

A. Divorce dissolves the matrimonial ties and terminates the marriage. However, judicial separation does not terminate the marriage relationship but only modifies it by suspending for the time being the obligation to live together. Parties still have the option to reunite again, as the marriage is still subsisting. (Visit at: *http://divorceinindia.blogspot.com*)

Q9. What is the right of husband in custody of a child, after judicial separation/Divorce with wife?

A. As per the Guardian and Wards Act, 1890 and Hindu Minority and Guardianship Act, 1956 a Hindu father is recognized as the legal guardian of his male and unmarried female minor children in preference to the mother. Further, Section 19(b) of Guardian and Wards Act, 1890, says when the father is living, no one else can be appointed as guardian unless a father is found unfit to be a guardian. Therefore, after divorce/separation, the husband can move an application for the custody of a child under Guardian & wards Act and if the parties are Hindu then under Hindu Minority & Guardianship Act. The husband also has a right to claim the right of visitation/meeting the child and to take the child during holidays till the disposal of the petition for custody. The parties can ask for the above said interim relief from the Court.

Q10. **A couple wants to dissolve their marriage by taking divorce by mutual consent. A settlement deed has been prepared, which states that the Husband shall be transferring one of his houses in favour of wife in lieu of permanent alimony and maintenance? What is the procedure for obtaining mutual divorce? What short of transfer document needs to be prepared and is the same needs to be registered?**

A. The marriage can be dissolved by seeking divorce on mutual consent, which can be obtained under the provisions of Section 13 B of the Hindu Marriage Act, 1955. The prerequisite for a joint petition of divorce on mutual consent is that the husband and wife must be living separately and have not cohabitated together for a period of more than 1 year and further that inspite of their best efforts are not in position to live together any further.

The procedure for obtaining divorce by mutual consent involves filing of two successive petitions (First Motion and Second Motion Petitions) with consent, all through of both husband and wife for seeking divorce. The second motion petition can only be filed after expiry of the statutory period of six months from the first motion joint petition. The decree of divorce is granted by court after consent of both parties is recorded in the second motion petition. If any party withdraws the consent in between the statutory period or before giving consent in second motion, no divorce can be granted on that petition.

The transfer of house can be made as per the settlement deed in favour of the wife, as per the mode given in the settlement deed itself. However, since the consent can always be withdrawn by either of the spouse before the statement in second motion petition (i.e., within the period of six months), it is advisable to complete transaction when the consent statement is made in the second motion petition and the divorce decree is being granted. The transaction of an immovable property with a value of more than Rs.100/-, definitely needs registration with the Sub-Registrar. Since, there is no money consideration in the transfer of the property in favour of the wife, it would be better to make a Gift Deed on requisite stamp paper and register the same with the Sub-Registrar.

Q11. What is the difference between annulment of marriage and dissolution of marriage by divorce?

A. Under the provisions of Sec.11 of the Hindu Marriage Act, 1955, a marriage could be declared a nullity being void *ab-initio* (see Legal Glossary). A marriage is declared void if either party has a spouse living at the time of marriage; or parties are within the degree of prohibited relationship; or the parties are sapindas to each other. There are certain marriages which could also be annulled being voidable marriages under Sec.12 of the Act. However, in contrast to this a Divorce in relation to marriages, which were otherwise valid could be taken on the grounds specified under Section under Sec.13 of Hindu Marriage Act, 1955, which are as follows:

(a) If the other party after the marriage had voluntary sexual inter-course with any other person; or

(b) If the other party after marriage has treated the petitioner with cruelty; or

(c) If the other party has deserted the petitioner for a continuous period of not less than two years at the time of filing the petition; or

(d) If the other party has seized to be a Hindu by conversion to another religion; or

(e) If the other party has been incurably of unsound mind or has been suffering from mental disorder of such a kind and to such an extent that the petitioner cannot be reasonably expected to live with her/him; or

(f) If the other party has been suffering from an virulent and incurable form of leprosy; or

(g) If the other party has been suffering from venereal disease in a communicable form; or

(h) If the other party has renounced the world by entering into any religious order; or

(i) If the other party has not been heard of being alive for a period of seven years or more by persons who would have naturally heard of it; had that party being alive.

Divorce can also be obtained by mutual consent by Husband and Wife in terms of Section 13 B of the Hindu Marriage Act, 1955. A joint petition for seeking mutual divorce by consent under the above provision can be filed, subject to, that the parties to the petition must be living separately and have not cohabitated for a continuous period of more than one year and further are not able to live together any further.

Q12. Whether a wife has indefeasible right to claim maintenance under Sec.125 Cr.P.C.? Under what circumstances, such a right to claim maintenance can be challenged?

A. The Legislative intent of making the above provision is to avoid vagrancy of deserted wife and under Hindu Law a husband is under obligation to maintain his wife. However, there could be circumstances, where a wife can be legally refused for grant of maintenance. Apart from the fact, that the wife is financially independent and does not require maintenance; the grounds, which disentitle a wife to claim maintenance are:-

A). *Claim against Second Husband without divorcing the First Husband*: A wife marrying a second husband without first taking divorce from first husband has no right to claim maintenance from the second husband.

b). *Wife living in Adultery* : A wife living in adultery, as per Sub Sec.(4) & (5) of Sec.125 Cr.P.C. is not entitled to apply for maintenance allowance or from enforcing any maintenance order already granted against the husband.

c). *Wife Refusing to Live with Husband*: Where in the absence of reasonable cause, a wife refuses to live with the husband makes third ground disentitling the wife to claim maintenance.

d). *Wife living separately by Mutual consent*: Where the couple entered into an agreement to live separately by mutual consent and starts living separately, accordingly. In such circumstances, a wife is not entitled to claim maintenance.

CHAPTER 7

LABOUR & INDUSTRIAL DISPUTES

CHAPTER 7

LABOUR & INDUSTRIAL DISPUTES

Q1. **A running cinema is being closed down on account of demolition of the entire building and the workmen have been asked to leave and settle their accounts. Whether termination of workmen on account of closure of the establishment amounts to "retrenchment", if yes, to what amount of compensation the workmen are entitled to?**

A. After the enactment of S.25-FF and S.25 - FFF of Industrial Disputes Act, "retrenchment" includes every kind of termination of service except those not expressly included in S.25-F or not expressly provided for by other provisions of the Act such as Ss.25-FF and 25-FFF. The explanation to Sec.25-FFF, clearly says that closure on account of financial difficulty, loss of business would not attract compensation of three month salary, as the same cannot be treated as closure due to unavoidable circumstances. The same would amount to retrenchment and compensation under Sec.25-F at the rate of 15 days average pay for every completed year of service while calculating their period of service up to the date of closure is legally payable to the workmen.

Q2. **A workmen was granted loan of Rs.12,500/-**

and later had also received an advance of Rs.1500/-. The loan was to be repaid by deduction from the salary and Rs.5000/- has already been deducted. However, the workmen left the services without settling the account. Can the loan and advance be deducted from the Gratuity amount payable to the workmen and how Gratuity is to be computed?

A. Gratuity is a retirement benefit for the past service of the employee; and like pension and provident fund, it cannot be adjusted for loan and advances. An employee does not contribute any portion of his salary towards this amount. Gratuity under the Payment of Gratuity Act, 1972 is also not liable to be attached in execution of any decree or order of a civil, revenue or criminal court. The said protection is given by Sec.13 of the Act. However, if the employee has agreed to the deduction of an amount out of gratuity due then that amount can be deducted. **(Jaganatha Dasik Vs. Bina Khadi & Village Industries Board; 1995 Lab. IC. 923)**

The computation method of Gratuity:

The Gratuity is applicable only on completion of five continuous years of service and is calculated at rate of 15 days of wages on the last drawn salary for each completed year of service. The monthly wage is divided by 26 and multiplied by 15. In computation of a completed year, period above six months shall be treated as a full year.

Gratuity= Basic Monthly Salary + Dearness Allowance/26 **X** 15days **X** No. of years of Service

Q.3. I am a workmen in a factory and my services were terminated without any cause. What are the benefits to which I am entitled to? Can I challenge my illegal termination in the labour court directly without reference from the Central Government?

A. Sec.10(4) of the Industrial Disputes Act talks about a reference being made by the Central Government for reference of any industrial dispute in the labour court or Tribunal. It was a mandatory provision and therefore, no direct challenge could be made by a workmen against discharge, dismissal, retrenchment or otherwise termination of service before a labour court or tribunal.

However, with the latest amendment in the Act w.e.f. 15th September, 2010, the workmen can directly make an application before labour court or tribunal after the expiry of 3 months from the date of making application before conciliation officer of Central Government for conciliation of dispute. The amendment further put a limitation to file such application directly in the labour court or tribunal within 3 years from the date of such termination.

The workmen is entitled to retrenchment benefits under Sec.25(f) of the Act, gratuity, if applicable and all other statutory benefits from the employer in case of termination of service.

CHAPTER 8

MISCELLANEOUS

CHAPTER 8

MISCELLANEOUS

Q1. I want to purchase a benami property in the name of my son and my unmarried daughter. Is it legally permissible to do so?

A. Sec. 4 of Benami Transactions (Prohibition) Act, clearly bars any benami transaction and also the right to claim back the property held benami. Thus, Benami transactions are prohibited under the law. However, a property purchased by you for the benefit of your wife or unmarried daughter is not affected by the aforesaid provision.

Q2. What is Mediation and how it works?

A. "Peace is not the absence of conflict but the ability to deal with it", as said by Ghandi ji.

Mediation is an Alternative Dispute Resolution Process. It is a Structured informal Negotiation Process in which a neutral third party i.e. Mediator facilitates the disputants to arrive at a settlement beneficial for both parties, which is called a `win-win position' to end the conflict. The entire process is voluntary, confidential, transparent and flexible. The process provides an opportunity to both the parties to explain the issues. The information provided to the Mediator is to help him understand the points of agreement and disagreement. In the next phase i.e., resolving the Conflict, the Mediator uses certain skills and techniques thereby guiding the parties from conflict to settlement.

Finally, the settlement agreement is drafted by the Mediator. Mediation is more beneficial, as it is more accessible and less adversarial, expensive and time consuming, and more likely to bring result that is matching the interest of the disputants.

Q3. What is an FIR?

A. It is the first hand information given to the police regarding any cognizable offence, which may or may not include the names of offenders. It is the first step, which bring the criminal law into motion.

Q4. What is Domestic violence and what are salient features of "The Protection of Women from Domestic Violence Act, 2005"? Whether `live-in relationship' has been covered under the present Act and who could be a respondent in a complaint filed under the Act?

A. A domestic violence is also a Human Right Violence. Domestic Violence occurs when one of the adult members in domestic relationship tries to take control of the relationship. It could be psychological or emotional abuse or typical physical abuse.

The Protection of Women from Domestic

Violence Act 2005, is applicable to women and children in domestic relationship and provide protection to women who are legally married and also those who are in live-in relationship, women who are sisters, widows or mother. It also provides a right to reside in the matrimonial and shared household, whether or not she has any legal title in the household. The most important aspect of this Act is the recognition of Economic Violence, like not providing money, food, clothes, medicines; Causing hindrance to employment opportunities; Forcing a woman to vacate her house; Not paying rent etc. A complaint under Sec.12 of the Act can filed against persons who are in domestic relationship. Section 2 (q) says that any adult male member who has been in a domestic relationship with the aggrieved person is the 'respondent'. The respondent can also be a relative of the husband or male partner – thus, a father-in-law, mother-in-law, or even siblings of the husband and other relatives can be proceeded against.

Q5. **I with my wife want to adopt a child from a Child Agency/Child Homecare for orphan children. What are the pre-requisites and how to go about it?**

A. The in country adoption is governed by CARA (Child Adoption Resource Agency) guidelines and you have to first register yourself with a Specialised Adoption Agency. The agency would be scrutinizing your medical fitness record and sound financial status by Home Study report. After registration with the

Agency, you will have the chance to adopt a child depending upon availability of the child and in the order of priority on the basis of registration of other proposed adopted parents. Once, successful matching is done; the agency will file a formal application in the competent court i.e., District Judge, for grant of adoption certificate/order. The child can be legally placed in adoption under the provisions of Juvenile Justice (care and protection of children) Act, 2000 or Hindu Adoption and Maintenance Act (HAMA).

LEGAL GLOSSARY

Award : It means interim or final determination of any dispute under Arbitration Act and conciliation Act, 1996 or Industrial Disputes Act.

District Court : Principal Civil court of a notified district having jurisdiction over the area.

Judge : Officer Presiding the court having judicial or quasi-judicial functions.

Suit : Claim of a civil nature.

Plaintiff : One who present a plaint (lawsuit) for seeking a relief from the court.

Defendant : Party against which an action is brought for seeking a particular relief.

Written Statement: Also known as Statement of Defendant, which is also part of pleading thereby giving reply to the points made in the plaint. It is also known as `Jawab Dawa' i.e., Reply to the claim.

Injunction : Restraint order passed by civil court against a person to refrain from doing some overt or covert act.

Application : It has not been defined in Code of Civil Procedure and General Clauses Act, however, it means `a request, oral or in writing'. It also includes a petition.

Rent Controller : Presiding Officer of a Tribunal under Rent Control Act having judicial function, but is not a court in strict sense.

Bailee : on whom personal property is entrusted for a particular purpose, like a common carrier.

Will : A testamentary document bequeathing rights in the property of the testator to the persons in whose favour will is executed.

Codicil : Codicil has been derived from a latin word `codicillus'. Codicil means a Supplement or Appendix to the main will. It amends, modifies, add, alter, explain or revokes the existing will or part of it.

Ex-parte : A judicial proceeding conducted in the absence of one party and for the benefit of other is called Ex-parte. The party proceeded exparte can always join the proceeding, however, in case of any adverse order being passed against him, he can apply for setting aside exparte order to relegate back to the same position as on the date of passing of exparte order.

Sine-die Adjournment : Adjournment of the case to a date, which is not fixed. It does not terminate the proceedings and case is still pending with all interlocutory orders.

Evidence : Oral statement or a document to corroborate and/or prove existence of a fact.

Deposition : Oral statement by a witness

Fact : Statement of fact, which is proved by a cogent evidence. (Illustration: "Ram is clever". It is a statement of fact, which may or may not be correct.)

Burden of Proof : It is the duty of one party to a lawsuit to prove a disputed question of fact. One who alleges a statement of fact is in law is burdened with its proof. That initial burden to prove a disputed fact, never shifts on the other party.

Divorce : Judicial order terminating a marriage.

Judicial Seperation : Court order allowing the parties to marriage to live separately without terminating marriage.

Maintenance : Expenses to be paid to the other dependent spouse; or by adult independent children to aged parents for their upkeep.

Domestic Violence : All sort of psychological, emotional, physical and economic abuses carried upon women and children in domestic relationship to take control of the relationship.

Cohabitation : Act of living together and having sexual relationship (especially without getting married)

Reconciliation : To patch up without putting guilt for the past conduct and to pick up thread for a new life. It's peace building approach and is part of a less common approach, which is transformative or relationship centered often associated with Mediation Process.

Limitation : A statute of limitations is a law that dictates the period till when a right can be enforced in court of law; after expiry of limitation period the right may exist but the same cannot be enforced.

Court fees : Court fees Act, 1870 defines the costs of handling a lawsuit in the court of law to be paid by the plaintiff.

Issues : Disputed question of facts between the parties, which also includes legal question.

Wife : A women joined in marriage; and also include a woman who has been divorced or has obtained divorced, but not remarried.

Marriage : It differs from person to person. In Muslims it is a contract and under amended Hindu Marriage Act it is sacramental agreement.

Live-in Relation : A living arrangement between unmarried couple for a long term relationship, which has a semblance with marriage.

Void : Agreements or contracts, which are not valid or enforceable being against the law.

Ab-initio : From the start.

Resjudicata	:	A mixed question of law and fact determined in the earlier proceeding between the same parties, for the same reason cannot be questioned in a subsequent proceeding between the same parties.

Framework of Indian Legal System:

India is a country of vast population and having a diversified ethnic culture and religions; beside Hindus in majority there are Muslims, Christian, Parsi etc. India became Federal Republic and the constitution of India came into force on 26th Jan., 1950. The constitution guarantees some fundamental rights to its citizens, such as, right to equality, freedom of expression, right to life and personal freedom, Right to religion, right to education and right to redress to the courts, etc.

Indian Judiciary is like a pyramid with Lower or District Courts at its bottom; and in the hierarchy High courts of states comes in the middle, and the Supreme Court at the top. The court system can be classified into civil courts, criminal courts and different Administrative Tribunals. Further, civil courts are divided into on the basis of pecuniary and territorial jurisdiction based on division of different districts. Similarly, Criminal courts are also Sub- divided into court of sessions and Metropolitan Magistrate. Each District Court is presided by a District Judge.

The High Courts and Supreme Court have mainly Appellate function and power to dispose petition involving violation of fundamental rights. However, some of the State High Courts also have functions of Original side, like in Delhi High Court. The Supreme Court has exclusive regulative powers of the Union and thus, can review orders/judgments of the High Courts and declare legislation as unconstitutional. Article 124 and 125 of the Indian Constitution ensures the independence of the judiciary.

The Indian legal system establishes the procedure and legal framework in order to dispense justice with all its fairness to all those who required justice. The laws basically are classified into two categories; a) Adjective or Procedural laws; and b). substantive laws. Substantive law gives remedies and rights, which can be enforced by using the adjective or procedural laws like, Code of Civil Procedure. However, of late it is realized that procedural law instead of paving way to achieve and subserve ends of justice is in fact, creating obstructions and delays, that is why inspite of its incalculable promise it is no more self-effectuating.

Acknowledgement

I tender my gratitude to my parents for the encouragement and support given all through. I must also thank my friend Ramneek Wig, who has inspired and helped me in the course of book writing.

My Mentor, Mr. Rajiv Bahl, Advocate has always been there to support and guide me and I would like to tender my sincere gratitude to him for showing me the way.

I would also like to thank my wife Beena for her immense emotional support.

www.ingramcontent.com/pod-product-compliance
Ingram Content Group UK Ltd.
Pitfield, Milton Keynes, MK11 3LW, UK
UKHW021410190726
13845UKWH00028B/1001

9 788192 496900